NOTHING!

Open them again.

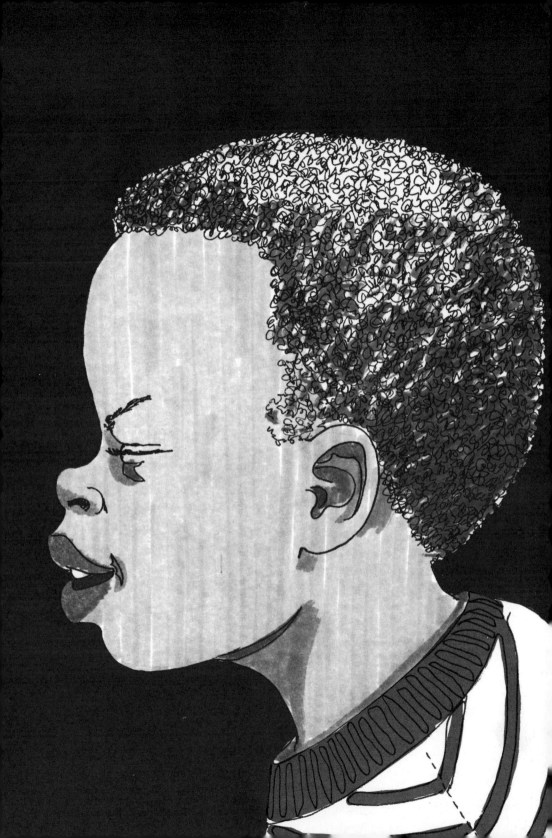

What can you see now?

Look at all
these things!

Cover your ears with
your hands.
Cover them tight!
Now, what do you hear?

NOTHING!

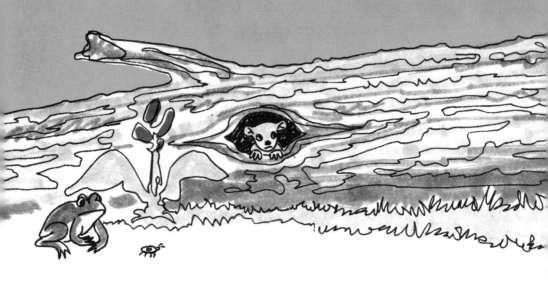

Uncover your ears and listen.

Have you heard these things?

Hide your hands. Sit
on them. Now, what do you
feel?

NOTHING MUCH!

Let your hands loose.
What can you feel now?

Are all
these
things
safe
to touch?

Hold your nose.
HOLD it real tight!
Now,
What do you smell?

NOTHING!

OK, let go of your
nose. Take your hands
away.

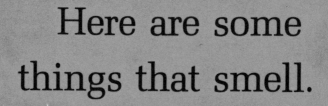

Here are some things that smell.

Close your mouth.
CLOSE it tight!
Now,
    what can you taste?

NOTHING!

OK, open it up. OPEN
YOUR MOUTH!

Now you can taste things like this.

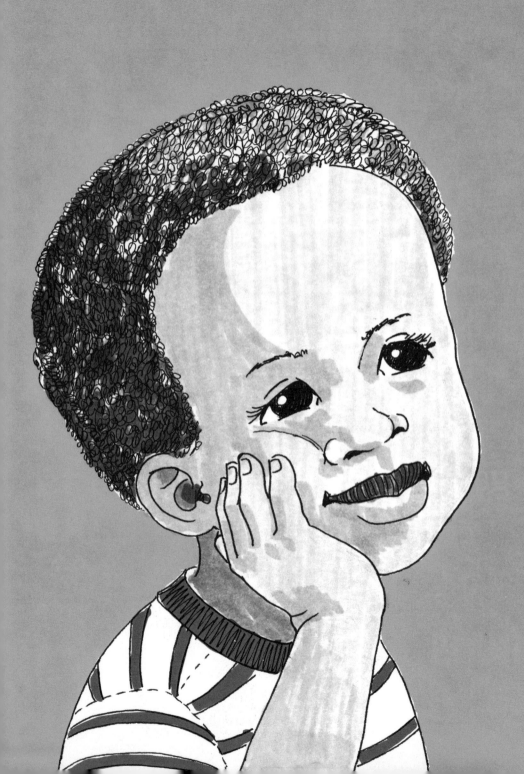

Think about these five little gifts you have.

You can taste. You can feel. You can smell, and you can hear things, too. And don't forget your eyes that see! Isn't it fun!

Our God is so good. He gave us all these things when He made us.

Now, aren't you glad He did?

But be careful! There are things never to be looked at, never to be heard, touched, or eaten. And there are things never to be smelled at all.

But, you don't do things that you shouldn't do, do you? Why, of course you don't! And you have made God so happy, because He knows that you will never ever want to.

As you looked on the pages of this book, did you find all the things listed here for you to look at? Now, if you didn't, just look again, and you will find every one of them. Here they are:

A maple tree seed, a bat and baseball, a parachute, bubbles, dandelion seeds, feathers, a balloon, a hummingbird, a paper airplane and an airplane, a wasp, leaves, a bee, paper, a butterfly, a pelican, a sea gull, a mosquito, a kite, a dragonfly, the sun, the moon, some stars, some clouds, a helicopter, and the sky.

Now, here are some more things that you should have found to look at:

A little ant, an acorn, grass, a toad, a pine cone, a penny, a ladybug, clover, a mouse, a turtle, a toadstool, a centipede, a rabbit, wood, a plant, a praying mantis, a grasshopper, a dandelion, a trillium flower, a spider and its web, wheat, a fence, a cow, a caterpillar, a deer, a tree, a squirrel, leaves, a hornet's nest, and a hole in a tree.

That was fun, wasn't it?

But now, did you find pictures of all these things for your ears to listen to? If not, then you had better look again. Here they are:

A squeaking mouse, and a buzzing bee, a singing mosquito, dripping water, a singing cicada, a cricket, a honking goose, a noisy baby bird, a pecking woodpecker, and a tree frog peeping.

And here are some more things that you should have found for your ears to hear:

A growling bear, a banging firecracker, a howling dog, a loud monkey, a hollering boy, a ticking clock that's ringing, a pounding hammer, clapping hands, a noisy horse, a mewing cat, a coin that fell, a ringing bell, lightning that makes thunder, a talking parrot, a loud cow, a calling chimp, a blowing whistle, a barking dog,